African Lions

by Joelle Riley

Lerner Publications Company • Minneapolis

Lerner Publications Company
A division of Lerner Publishing Group, Inc.
241 First Avenue North
Minneapolis, MN 55401 U.S.A.

Website address: www.lernerbooks.com

Words in *italic* type are explained in a glossary on page 30.

Library of Congress Cataloging-in-Publication Data

Riley, Joelle.
    African lions / by Joelle Riley.
        p.   cm. — (Pull ahead books)
    ISBN-13: 978-0-8225-6703-5 (lib. bdg. : alk. paper)
    ISBN-10: 0-8225-6703-2 (lib. bdg. : alk. paper)
        1. Lions—Juvenile literature. I. Title.
    QL737.C23R546 2008
    599.757—dc22   2006024166

Manufactured in the United States of America
1 2 3 4 5 6 — JR — 13 12 11 10 09 08

This animal is a lion.

What is the long hair around this lion's face called? The long hair is called a *mane*.

Adult male lions have manes.
But females don't.

A lion's body is covered with short,
yellowish brown hair.
How does this help lions?

Lions' hair matches the color of the grass. That helps lions hide.

Hiding helps lions sneak up on other animals.

Lions are *predators*. They hunt and eat other animals.

Lions usually hunt wildebeests, zebras, impalas, and waterbucks.

This animal
is an impala.
The animals
a lion hunts
are called its
prey.

Groups of female lions often hunt together. First, they find some prey.

The lions slowly move closer and closer to the animals.

Then the lion charges!

One of the lions knocks the
animal down. The lion bites the
animal to kill it.

Then the lions begin to eat. The
biggest, strongest lions eat first.
Baby lions eat after the adults.

Lions live in a group called a *pride*.

Female lions and their babies live close together.

Male lions stay nearby.

When two lions meet, they make a friendly puffing sound.

Then one of the lions rubs its head against the other lion.

Lions also meow, snarl, and make purring sounds.

And lions ROAR!

Roaring lions can be heard from miles away.

Sometimes lions in a pride
roar together.

Other lions that are far away
roar to answer them.

All adult lions roar. Baby lions try to roar too. But their voices aren't very loud. Baby lions are called *cubs*.

Female lions are called *lionesses*.
A lioness usually has two to four cubs.

Lion cubs are born in a *den*.

A den is a safe place hidden
behind rocks or bushes.

The cubs drink their mother's milk.
This is called *nursing*. The cubs
grow quickly.

The cubs wrestle and pounce. They
grow bigger and stronger.

The young lions watch
the adults hunt.

They learn what to do. Soon they
will be able to hunt too.

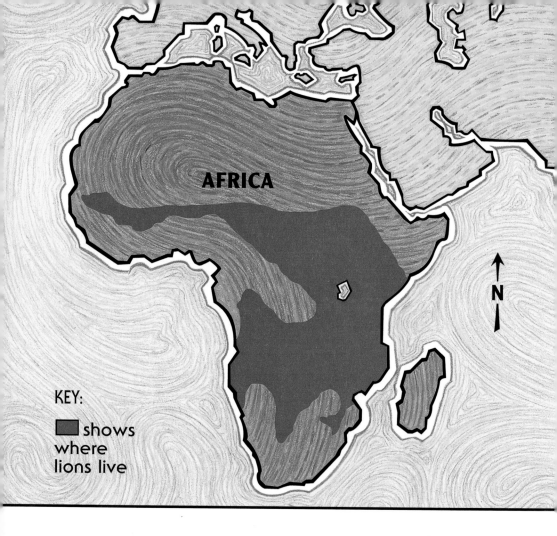

AFRICA

N

KEY:

█ shows
where
lions live

This is a map of Africa.
Where do African lions live?

Parts of a Lion's Body

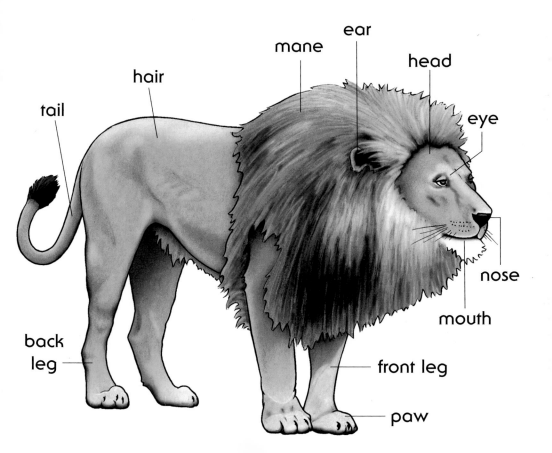

tail

hair

mane

ear

head

eye

nose

mouth

back leg

front leg

paw

Glossary

cubs: baby lions

den: a safe place where baby lions are born

lionesses: female lions

mane: the long hair around a male lion's face

nursing: drinking milk from a mother's body

predators: animals that hunt and eat other animals

prey: the animals lions hunt

pride: a group of lions that live together

Further Reading and Websites

African Lion (*Panthera leo krugeri*)
http://www.thebigzoo.com/Animals/African_Lion.asp

African Savanna
http://nationalzoo.si.edu/Animals/AfricanSavanna
/afsavskids.cfm

Donaldson, Madeline. *Africa*. Minneapolis: Lerner Publications Co., 2005.

Kendell, Patricia. *Lions*. Austin, TX: Raintree Steck-Vaughn, 2002.

Lions
http://www.nationalgeographic.com/kids
/creature_feature/0109/lions2.html

Seidensticker, John, and Susan Lumpkin. *Cats: Smithsonian Answer Book*. Washington, DC: Smithsonian Books, 2004.

Index

Photo Acknowledgments

The photographs in this book are used with the permission of: PhotoDisc Royalty Free by Getty Images, pp. 3, 9; © Getty Images, pp. 4, 12, 13, 14, 19; © Joe McDonald/Visuals Unlimited, p. 5; © Royalty-Free/CORBIS, pp. 6, 23; © Michele Burgess, pp. 7, 8, 10; © Martin Harvey/Peter Arnold, Inc., p. 11; © Michael Fairchild/Peter Arnold, Inc., p. 15; © John Conrad/CORBIS, p. 16; © Jeff Griffin/iStockphoto, p. 17; © J & B PHOTOGRAPHERS/Animals Animals, p. 18; © The Image Bank/Getty Images, p. 20; © David J Slater/Alamy, p. 21; © C & M Denis-Huot/Peter Arnold, Inc., p. 22; © Rich Kirchner, pp. 24, 26; © Gregory G. Dimijian/Photo Researchers, Inc., p. 25; U.S. Fish and Wildlife Service, p. 27.

Front Cover: © Fritz Polking/Visuals Unlimited.